HAPPY VEGAN COMFORT FOOD

Karoline Jönsson

PAVILION

KAROLINE JÖNSSON

—

I'd like to start this book by being completely honest with you and confessing that from 2012 to 2014 I was actually quite hungry. These were my first two years as a vegan and I was lost in the spinach.

Of course, it's not true that you can't get full from plant-based food or that the body won't feel satisfied and happy. But for me, who previously had often used the trinity of meat, sauce and potato as a starting point, it was sometimes difficult and time-consuming to translate this into a diet based on plants. Moreover, I had just discovered my new great interest in cooking and was therefore enthusiastically trying out different crazy ingredients, flavour combinations and other concoctions. Sometimes it turned out well but often the result was just so-so. Vegetable fritters often had a soft, crumbling texture, and nutritious filling pulses (legumes) hadn't yet become a staple in my diet.

But then something happened. Because during those two years I came to understand this new cuisine and learn new ways to compose meals – and above all, how to cook good everyday vegan food. I had picked up a repertoire of dishes that I could master, that always turned out delicious and filling and

that I could come back to week after week. From these fail-proof recipes I was able to use the concept, cooking methods and flavour combinations to develop new dishes, and from then on, a whole new world of food opened its doors for me.

Looking back, I wish that I had had access to good recipes during that time instead of having to improvise every day. But even though it's not that long ago, the vegan world looked completely different then. The interest in plant-based food was still in its infancy and it was significantly harder to find good vegan products and dinner inspiration, as well as vegan food when eating out.

Happy Vegan Comfort Food is the book that I needed when I decided to quit eating animals. It would have saved me years of finding my way in the green jungle. In a way, this might be my most personal book so far, because here you really are invited to my table to enjoy dinner, breakfast and snacks. I've gathered together the food that we always come back to at home. The dishes that always work, always taste good and that we always crave: food that is filling and that warms the soul and the heart – happy vegan comfort food!

VEGAN COMFORT FOOD

from apple picking to rhubarb buds

—

I live in an old house in the countryside in southern Sweden. It's on a small hill with a rolling landscape of fields and horse pastures that border our little farm. In October when the autumn storms arrive, the wind from the West rages so that the roof creaks and a draught comes up between the floorboards.

Everyone I know who lives like this – in an old house in the countryside – gets up every morning, lights a fire in at least one stove and then feeds the fire with logs until it's time to go to bed again. Otherwise it's cold. So if anyone should write a book about warming comfort food, it feels right that it should be one of us country folk who often wakes up with a cold nose or walks around in woolly socks every day for four months in a row. For me it's a given that food and drink should be warming from the inside out during the cold season.

Here, far up in the north, we live in a climate with distinct seasonal changes. When I first started to develop recipes for this book I had autumn in mind, thinking about the food you'd want to eat when it starts getting darker and you snuggle up indoors while the rain is drumming on the window and the wind is whistling outside. But I soon realised that these recipes are also useful throughout winter… and to put it bluntly, it's actually pretty cold until May.

For eight months each year, between apple picking and seeing the first rhubarb buds, we are exposed to cold weather, wind and darkness, and our appetite for warming food intensifies. Around September I tend to notice that I'm no longer satisfied with new potato salads dressed with lemon vinaigrette or steamed summer veg with a dollop of dairy-free butter. This is when I start to crave spicy stews, hearty soups and roasted root vegetables dunked in rich mayonnaise. Food should no longer be light and cooling for the summer heat, but instead should fulfil the opposite function – warming up a cold body.

It's rather curious that our vegetables seem to follow the same cycle. The bursting-with-chlorophyll vegetables that sprout up when the spring sun starts to cast its warming rays in April don't need a lot of cooking, just a light frying or steaming, or can even be eaten raw. Then we eat our way through summer with lots of fresh food. But when autumn arrives the root vegetables have just grown big enough, and it's time to dig up the potatoes, store the pumpkins and hang the onions up to dry. These ingredients will see us through the autumn and winter months, when they take on that hearty character the body is craving. Isn't it fantastic how everything seems to be linked together?

The recipes in this book are designed to be adaptable – you can vary the ingredients and you will soon start to develop your own dishes. For successful everyday cooking it helps if you're able to be spontaneous and flexible in the kitchen. Therefore you will see that I've suggested alternative ingredients for many of the recipes. This means that the dishes can change with the seasons and can be made even if you weren't able to buy a specific ingredient.

The ability to be flexible in the kitchen means that you will get to eat more varied food while minimising waste. It will also make you a better cook. And since my aim is to help everyone to cook such delicious plant-based food that animal products are redundant, this chapter begins with a lesson in composing a plant-based meal.

THE PLANT-BASED KITCHEN

BALANCE
the basic tastes

Food that is full of flavour – that includes most of the five basic taste elements – is complex and is perceived by the eater as satisfying. But perhaps the biggest challenge when creating recipes is that it's often the little details that make all the difference. Just a gram of salt can determine whether a whole meal is enhanced or just tastes OK. And as if that wasn't tricky enough, we all have different taste preferences.

I once sat in an award-winning restaurant, took my first bite of food and thought 'Damn, that's salty,' just as my dining partner said 'Oops, they've forgotten the salt.' I laughed as he reached for the salt and started sprinkling.

Having said that, it doesn't matter how well written recipes are if the person doing the cooking doesn't engage with and take time to taste the food. And this is one of the best things about eating your own food – it's fully tailored to your own taste. So if you're hunched over the pot with the tasting spoon in your mouth and don't immediately think 'Wow!', consider the following:

> — What brings acidity to the dish? Is it enough or do you need to add a squeeze of lemon or lime juice, for example?
> — Have you added anything sweet? This could, for example, come from root vegetables, onion, or cranberry sauce.
> — Does the dish have enough umami? How would a little bouillon powder or a tablespoon of tamari affect it?
> — Is it salty enough?
> — Would something bitter enhance the dish? Perhaps in the form of coffee or fresh lingonberries that cut through a sweet dessert, or a handful of rocket (arugula) added to a stew.

VARY
the textures

A truly satisfying meal needs a variety of textures. Eating a smooth soup or mashed potato together with equally mushy bean fritters means that you just spoon away the dinner until all of a sudden it's gone.

If, instead, you put together a meal that has several different textures – for example crisp lettuce, creamy sauce, crunchy nuts, chewy goji berries, soft steamed vegetables, crispy fritters, smooth hummus – the meal will offer a variety of textures, as well as flavours, which will make it feel more vibrant, interesting and satisfying.

This is especially important to keep in mind when your dinner has only a few components, for example when serving soup. Serving sauerkraut or finely shredded fennel with a soup will add freshness and give you something to chew. If you also include crunchy seeds, chewy bread and aromatic coriander (cilantro) or parsley, you have introduced several different textures to a simple dish. The meal will be perceived as much more interesting, and will also look beautiful.

Another thing to keep in mind is how the various components of a meal complement each other, both in texture and flavour. The soup doesn't necessarily have to have any acidity in it if you serve it with sauerkraut, for example, which will make an umami-packed soup seem even tastier.

If possible, make space for a little topping section in your cupboard, where you keep nuts, seeds, dried berries, berry or vegetable powders, and other things to sprinkle over soups, salads or porridge. When you buy different seeds, pour some into a jar to create your own mixed seeds. Don't toast them: it's best to do so just before serving them, as they will last longer and keep their nutritional value.

ADD
umami

One of the most important things when cooking plant-based food is to learn to add umami ('savouriness'). It sort of comes as a bonus when cooking with meat, but it's not difficult to get it right without animal products. One simple way to achieve this is to create a browned surface on your food by frying or roasting. Caramelised onion, fried mushrooms, celery or celeriac make a good flavour base for soups, stews, or a lentil mince. On the same principle, I have made it a habit to roast soup vegetables in the oven before blending them together with stock.

In the plant kingdom you will find umami flavours in ingredients such as tamari or Japanese soy sauce, miso paste, tahini, woody herbs such as sage, thyme and rosemary, lovage, celery and celeriac, mushrooms, caramelised onion, garlic, cumin, caraway, stock and broth, bay leaf, tomato purée (tomato paste), sun-dried tomatoes, roasted nuts, fermented foods and nutritional yeast.

CHOOSE
your protein

Some protein is found in flour, pasta and potatoes, but to get adequate nutrition it's essential to incorporate ingredients with a higher protein content in your plant-based diet. Pulses (legumes) are a simple way to add protein. It's great if you can include them in most meals, but think beyond hummus and bean salad – use bean-based pasta, add gram (chickpea/garbanzo) flour to fritters or a vegan 'omelette', blend cooked beans or lentils into a soup, add green beans to a hash or stir edamame (green soybeans) into a salad. Other ingredients rich in protein are buckwheat, quinoa, peanuts, almonds, and pumpkin, sunflower and hemp seeds.

17

STORE CUPBOARD STAPLES
that make a difference

Tamari – A fermented soy sauce that is rich in umami and has a pleasing saltiness. When there's a little something missing from a dish, I usually add a tablespoon of tamari to increase the umami and broaden the basic flavours.

Nutritional yeast – Contains B vitamins and adds a slightly cheesy flavour, for example to pasta sauces and creamy dishes. It can be blended together with cashew nuts for a Parmesan-like powder to sprinkle over pasta dishes when serving.

Chickpea flour – Also known as gram flour, garbanzo flour or besan, this is a super ingredient for adding more protein to your food. Excellent as a binding agent in vegetable fritters, it will give them a better texture than if you use blended beans. Chickpea flour gives a light and fluffy texture to pancakes and omelette-like dishes (such as the tortilla on page 62) and contains double the amount of protein of regular wheat flour.

Lemon juice – Vinegar can bugger off; nothing beats the acidity from the best fruit in the world – the lemon. Make sure you always have lemon juice at home: if it gets too expensive to use fresh lemons, you can buy organic lemon juice in a bottle. Bottled lemon juice is pasteurised and therefore heated, but if you're using it for dashing into a stew, even fresh lemon juice would get heated up enough to lower its nutritional value.

Tahini – Can be used to make fresh sauces and is nice to dip apple wedges into when you fancy a little snack.

Aquafaba – Aquafaba is the water that pulses (legumes) have been cooked in; when you buy canned pulses it is the liquid you drain off. You can also save the water if you boil your own pulses, but if you do, make sure not to use too much water when boiling. Aquafaba works in the same way as an egg for baking, and can also be used for making mayonnaise or as a binding agent in veg fritters. The best, most viscous, aquafaba comes from chickpeas (garbanzos) or white beans.

Beans – Buy big packs of dried beans and chickpeas (garbanzos), boil them in your largest pan and freeze in portion sizes, saving the cooking liquid. That way you will always have beans to hand for stews and soups as well as aquafaba for baking. Dried soya beans can be used to make your own tofu (see recipe on page 24). Mung beans have a shorter soaking and cooking time than larger beans and are my favourite to sprout.

Lentils – There are many different types of lentils, used in a wide variety of dishes. I always have red lentils, Puy lentils and beluga lentils at home. Unlike beans, lentils don't need soaking, which means that you don't always have to plan so carefully in advance. Red lentils will very easily turn to pulp when cooked and are therefore good for mince or in soups, while Puy and beluga lentils keep their shape well and are suitable for salads or when you want more texture.

Onion – I'd recommend that you start thinking of onion as a spice rather than as a vegetable and cook it in a way that brings out its sweet and umami qualities. Caramelise onion by frying it slowly over a low heat until it is soft and golden brown.

Salt – A good-quality sea salt or Himalayan salt has a milder saltiness than refined salt. This may sound like a small thing but it will actually make a big difference. All my recipes use natural salt, so if you use refined salt you might have to decrease the amount slightly.

Cumin – A cooking spice that I would like to champion: it is widely used in Middle Eastern cuisines. When I want to make a stew especially savoury and warming, cumin is usually my starting point.

Liquid smoke – In my early days as a vegan I particularly missed smoked food. When I discovered liquid smoke – water that has been smoked with hickory wood – it was easy to add smoked flavours to my food again. I use it when making seitan sausages (see page 34) and pulled jackfruit (see page 108), and add it to fried mushrooms to serve with dishes where I might once have added smoked bacon.

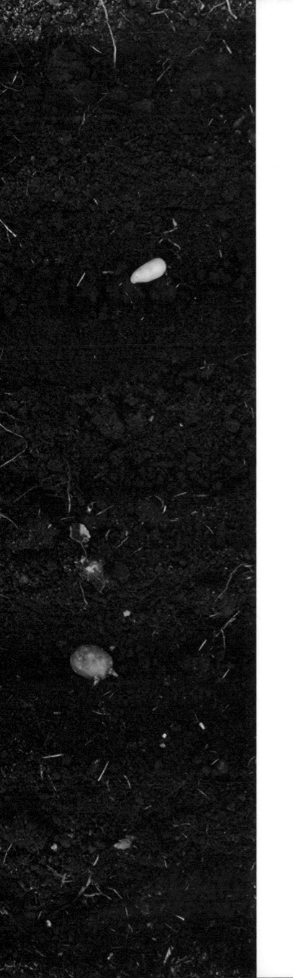

II

**FROM
SCRATCH**

HOME-MADE TOFU

—

Makes approx. 250g/9oz

280g/10oz/1½ cups dried
    soya beans
3½ tbsp apple cider
    vinegar

It's easy and cheap to make your own tofu, but there are several steps to go through so it takes a while to prepare. If you'd like to cook any of the tofu recipes in the book, you can of course use shop-bought tofu instead.

— Soak the soya beans for 12 hours.
— Drain off the water and rinse the beans. Place the beans in a blender together with 350ml/12fl oz/1½ cups water and blend until smooth. Meanwhile, bring 2 litres/3½ pints/ 2 quarts water to the boil in a large pan. When the water is boiling, add the bean mixture, bring back to the boil and then remove from the heat. Leave to rest for 5 minutes.
— Bring to the boil again and then remove from the heat. Strain the mixture through muslin (cheesecloth) into another pan, squeezing out as much liquid as possible. Put the bean pulp to one side and use later as soya mince (see page 28). Bring the liquid to the boil again, simmer for 10 minutes and then turn the heat off.
— In a clean pan, bring 300ml/10fl oz/1¼ cups water to the boil, remove from the heat and add the vinegar. Pour about one-third of the vinegar water into the soya milk and stir, then leave to rest for 5 minutes. Add another one-third and leave to rest for 5 minutes before adding the rest of the vinegar water. Now the soya milk will have curdled.
— Place a muslin-lined colander over a bowl and pour in the soya milk. Squeeze out as much of the liquid as possible and then place a weight over the bean cheese and leave for at least 30 minutes. I usually twist the muslin as tight as I can and leave the whole bundle in a colander with a pan filled with water on top.
— Transfer the finished tofu to a container together with a little of the squeezed-out liquid. Cover with a lid and store in the fridge. The tofu will keep fresh for about 1 week.

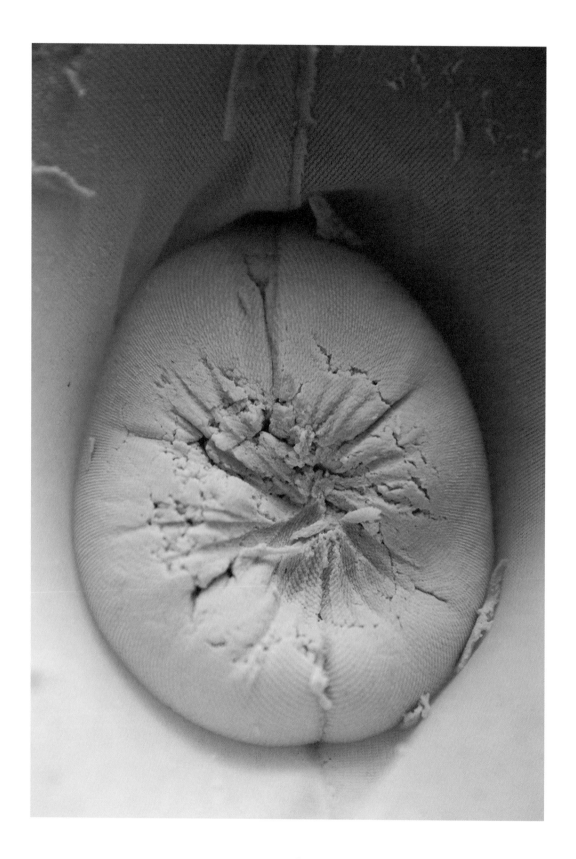

MINCE

—

In the plant-based kitchen you can make mince from various ingredients, such as pulses (legumes), nuts and seeds, and some of these minces are better suited for certain dishes. In the beginning it can be tricky to know which variety to choose for which dish, and you might prefer to stick to a shop-bought soya mince. Here are a few varieties to try if you'd like to make your own.

Soya mince

When making tofu (see page 24) you will have a large amount of bean pulp left over. This is called okara and it can be used as a kind of soya mince. It's more crumbly than the one you buy from the shops, but it's good for making falafel-type balls and I also use it as a base for bolognese. It can be a good idea to add other ingredients with more texture when you use home-made okara. If you search on the internet you will find plenty of recipes that use okara.

Lentil mince

Lentils are probably what I use the most for mince. I think lentil mince is the easiest base for all types of 'mince sauces', such as bolognese, chilli (see page 105), shepherd's pie (see page 129) and similar dishes.

SUNFLOWER SEED MINCE

—

Serves 4

120g/4oz/generous ¾
  cup sunflower seeds
1 large brown onion,
  roughly chopped
20g/¾oz/scant ½ cup
  fresh breadcrumbs
2 tbsp tamari
2 tbsp rapeseed (canola)
  oil, plus extra for frying
2 tbsp psyllium husk
salt and white pepper

This is one of my favourite types of mince. Sunflower seeds are an affordable ingredient and the mince is quick to rustle up without any soaking or other preparation. I use sunflower mince to make patties or balls.

— Blitz the sunflower seeds in a food processor or blender to make a coarse flour.
— Add the onion and blend until the onion is finely chopped.
— Scoop the mixture into a bowl, add the other ingredients and stir thoroughly. Season to taste, using a generous amount of salt. Shape into balls or patties and fry in oil until browned all over.

SEITAN

—

Seitan is made from wheat gluten and is a vegan meat alternative that is often used when you want to make dishes that are similar to ham, ribs or steak. Here, I use it for making chorizo and chunks that can be used in stews where you want a nice chunky texture.

For me, it's not so much that I'd like something that reminds me of meat, but rather because I want to recreate my old favourite dishes without using animal products.

Serves 8

1 shallot
1 small garlic clove
400g/14oz cooked white beans
5 tbsp tamari or light soy sauce
3 tbsp tomato purée (tomato paste)
1 tsp salt
1 tsp black pepper
1 tbsp paprika
1 tbsp lemon juice
500g/1lb 2oz/4 cups wheat gluten flour
500ml/17fl oz/2 cups vegetable stock

Stew chunks

— Preheat the oven to 180°C/350°F/Gas 4.
— Put all the ingredients, except the wheat gluten and stock, into a food processor or blender, add 200ml/7fl oz/ generous ¾ cup water and blend to a thick purée.
— Place the wheat gluten in a large bowl. Add the purée and stir until you have a firm dough. Tip out onto a work surface and knead the dough for 1 minute. Flatten it out to about 3cm/1¼in thick and place in a baking dish. Bake for 25 minutes.
— Bring the stock to the boil in a pan, pour into the baking dish and bake for a further 30 minutes. For the best result, flip the seitan over after about 15 minutes.
— Leave to cool, then cut or tear the seitan patty into bite-sized chunks.

Makes 8 sausages

½ brown onion
2 garlic cloves
400g/14oz cooked white
    beans
200ml/7fl oz/generous ¾
    cup vegetable stock
3 tbsp tamari
3 tbsp tomato purée
    (tomato paste)
1 tsp salt
1 tsp black pepper
1 tsp cayenne pepper
1 tbsp paprika
½–1 tsp liquid smoke
400g/14oz/3¼ cups
    wheat gluten flour

Chorizo

— Put all the ingredients, except the wheat gluten, into a food processor or blender and blend to a thick purée.
— Place the wheat gluten in a large bowl. Add the purée and stir until you have a firm dough. Tip out onto a work surface and knead for 1 minute. Divide the dough into eight pieces and use your hands to roll each piece into a sausage shape. Wrap each sausage in foil and twist the ends.
— Steam the sausages over a pan of boiling water for about 20 minutes, then remove from the heat and leave to cool. Remove the foil and store the sausages in the fridge or freezer until you are ready to use them. They will keep for at least a couple of days in the fridge.

BREAD ROLLS

—

8–10 rolls

10g/⅓oz fresh yeast (or
    about 5g/⅛oz dried)
400g/14oz/scant 3 cups
    strong white bread
    flour, plus extra for
    rolling out
½ tbsp salt

This is my go-to recipe when I want hot dog buns, burger buns or freshly baked breakfast rolls.

— Pour 300ml/10fl oz/1¼ cups cold water into a large mixing bowl and stir in the yeast. Add the flour and salt and quickly work into a dough. Cover the bowl with cling film (plastic wrap) or a damp tea towel and leave the dough to rise overnight or for around 12 hours at room temperature.
— Using a dough scraper, tip the dough onto a floured work surface. To make hot dog buns, fold the dough and carefully press it out into a rectangle measuring about 15 x 30cm/6 x 12in, then cut into 10 strips. For burger buns or breakfast rolls, make a rectangle about 18 x 35cm/7 x 14in, halve the dough lengthwise and cut each half into four pieces.
— Line a baking sheet with baking parchment. Place the buns on the baking sheet, cover with a cloth and leave to prove for 20 minutes. Preheat the oven to 250°C/500°F/Gas 9.
— Bake for 12–15 minutes or until risen and golden brown. Leave to cool, uncovered, on a wire rack for a crispy crust.

34

SAUERKRAUT

—

Makes approx. 1kg/2¼lb

1kg/2¼lb white or red
     cabbage
1 apple (optional)
1 tbsp non-iodised salt

You will need a glass jar
     with a clip top and
     rubber seal that holds
     approx. 1.5 litres/
     2½ pints/1½ quarts

**A jar of sauerkraut in the fridge is a wonderful
standby. Add it to salads, eat it in a breakfast
sandwich together with a thick layer of hummus,
or use it in Korean pancakes (see page 65).**

**During the winter, I often use sauerkraut to replace
leafy greens and sandwich veg that aren't in
season. Sauerkraut is a fantastic salad; the cabbage retains all its nutritional value and actually
becomes even more nutritious when it's fermented.
It will keep for several months in the fridge.**

— Wash your hands and thoroughly clean a large bowl and the
glass jar. Finely shred the cabbage, but save one cabbage
leaf. Grate the apple, if using. Place the cabbage and apple
in the bowl, add the salt and knead the cabbage for 15
minutes or until it's oozing with liquid.
— Pack the cabbage tightly into the jar and pour over the
liquid from the bowl. Place the cabbage leaf on the top to
keep the cabbage submerged in the liquid. If there is space
left in the jar, you can take a freezer bag and place it in the
jar, pour water into the bag until it reaches the top of the jar
and then tie the bag with a knot. If you use a bag you won't
need a cabbage leaf.
— Clip the lid onto the jar, making sure that the plastic bag (if
you're using one) doesn't protrude. Leave the jar to stand at
room temperature, out of direct sunlight, for 2 weeks. Then
transfer to the fridge.

BOUILLON POWDER

📷 page 43

Makes approx. 170g/6oz/¾ cup

5 leaves of kale, cavolo nero or leaves from, for example, kohlrabi, broccoli or cauliflower

1 handful beetroot (beet) tops or chard

4 parsnips

1 small celeriac (celery root) or ⅓ of a large one, or 5 celery stalks

2 brown onions with tops

5 garlic cloves

2 large sprigs of fresh lovage

3 tbsp fresh thyme leaves

3 tbsp chopped fresh sage

Home-made bouillon powder is relatively easy to make and will keep for a whole season, so take the opportunity to make a large batch at the beginning of autumn when many vegetables are cheap and taste their best. Alternatively, if you are growing your own you might have a surplus of crops in the vegetable patch – or you can use vegetables that you have thinned out, tops, leaves and herb sprigs: nothing need be wasted.

You can of course buy bouillon powder, which varies in quality from very good to merely adequate, but if you want to avoid additives, why not make your own? You don't have to be too strict about using the vegetables listed here, but it's good to include herbs, onion and celery or celeriac; and especially the great old heritage plant lovage, which is easy to grow and which packs in the most savoury flavour you can imagine.

— Rinse and clean the leaves and tops. Scrub the root vegetables with a vegetable brush. Cut everything into chunks.
— Blitz the ingredients in a food processor until everything is finely chopped.
— Spread out on a baking sheet lined with baking parchment and dehydrate in the oven at its lowest possible setting (50–70°C/120–160°F). Alternatively, dry in a dehydrator on a piece of baking parchment cut to shape. Make cuts in the paper and dollop out the bouillon mixture. The dehydrating will take around 1 day in an oven, 2 days in a dehydrator.
— Grind the dehydrated vegetables into a fine powder using a pestle and mortar and store in a lidded glass jar in a cool, dark, dry place.

CHILLI SAUCE

📷 page 43

**Makes approx.
300ml/10fl oz/1¼ cups**

15–20 red chillies
½ brown onion, thinly
   sliced
4 garlic cloves, thinly
   sliced
1 tbsp non-iodised salt

You will need a glass jar
   with a clip top and
   rubber seal that holds
   approx. 1 litre/
   1¾ pints/4 cups

Just like sauerkraut, this chilli sauce is fermented. It makes the sauce keep for longer while retaining, or even improving, the nutritional value of the vegetables. You can use this sauce in any recipe where I suggest using sriracha sauce.

— Wash the chillies, remove the seeds and cut into chunks.
— Place the chillies, onion, garlic and salt in the glass jar and add 300–400ml/10–14fl oz/about 1¼ cups water – enough to cover the vegetables. Stir until the salt has dissolved.
— If there is space left in the jar, you can take a freezer bag and place it in the jar, pour water into the bag until it reaches the top of the jar and then tie the bag with a knot. Clip the lid onto the jar, making sure that the plastic bag (if you're using one) doesn't protrude. Leave the jar to stand at room temperature, out of direct sunlight, for 2 weeks.
— Drain off the liquid, reserving some of it. Blend the vegetables in a food processor or blender and add 1 tablespoon of liquid at a time until you're happy with the consistency of the sauce. Pour it into a bottle and keep it in the fridge; it will keep for months.

TARRAGON MAYO

CHILLI MAYO

LEMON MAYO

MAYONNAISE

—

Serves 4

3 tbsp unsweetened soya milk without added calcium
100ml/3½fl oz/scant ½ cup rapeseed (canola) oil
1 tsp lemon juice
1 tsp Dijon mustard or Skånsk mustard
salt and black pepper

The amount of rapeseed (canola) oil that flows through my kitchen is typical of this part of Sweden. We fill our boots with rapeseed, and I usually eat mayonnaise at least once a week. The basic recipe can be flavoured in various ways. Lemon mayonnaise is particularly good with fresh vegetable dishes while the tarragon mayo makes a delicious dip for baked potato wedges. The chilli mayo is perfect when you want to add a slight heat to your food while the aioli is the best choice when you can't get enough of garlic.

— Blend all the ingredients together using a stick blender until you get a thick mayonnaise. If you want to use any of the flavourings, add the extra ingredients before blending.
— If the mayonnaise gets too thick you can whisk in a little more milk; if it feels too thin you can add more oil and blend for longer.

1 batch mayonnaise
1 tsp dried tarragon

Tarragon mayo

___

1 batch mayonnaise
1 tsp sriracha or other chilli sauce

Chilli mayo

___

1 batch mayonnaise
grated zest of ½ lemon, plus 1 tsp extra lemon juice

Lemon mayo

___

1 batch mayonnaise
1 large garlic clove, or more if you prefer, crushed

Aioli

___

45

PLANT DAIRY
—

**Makes approx.
800ml/28fl oz/
3 1/3 cups**

75g/2½oz/¾ cup
   rolled oats
800ml/28fl oz/3⅓ cups
   water
pinch of salt

**Makes approx.
1 litre/1¾ pints/
4 cups**

75g/2½oz/¾ cup
   rolled oats
60g/2oz/scant ½ cup
   sunflower seeds
1 litre/1¾ pints/4 cups
   water
pinch of salt
1 pitted date

**Makes approx.
500ml/17fl oz/
2 cups**

75g/2½oz/¾ cup
   rolled oats
500ml/17fl oz/2 cups
   water
pinch of salt

Plant-based 'dairy' products can be made from many seeds, grains and nuts, but here are some of the oat-based alternatives that I turn to the most.

Standard oat milk

Inexpensive milk that is quick to blend together and perfect for using in baking and cooking. If you are only using it for baking it's not necessary to strain it to remove the pulp.

Oat drink

This oat drink can also be used for baking or cooking. In addition, I like to use it for chia pudding or served with porridge or compotes.

Oat single (light) cream

Oat cream lends itself perfectly to creamed vegetables, pasta sauces or béchamel sauce. It can also be diluted with water to replace oat drink and is therefore practical to keep in the fridge.

— Blend all the ingredients together (preferably using a high-power blender) and leave to steep for a while, about 1 hour.
— Blend again for 1 minute. Strain through muslin (cheesecloth) and pour into a bottle.
— Store in the fridge. These will keep for about 5 days.

III

IN THE
FRYING PAN

RAGGMUNKAR/ SWEDISH POTATO PANCAKES

Makes 11–12

Potato pancakes

800g/1¾lb firm
    potatoes, peeled and
    finely grated
100g/3½oz/¾ cup plain
    (all-purpose) flour or
    sifted spelt flour
1 tsp salt
1 tsp baking powder
300ml/10fl oz/1¼ cups
    plant milk

Mushroom and onion topping

3 brown onions, thinly
    sliced
10 chestnut (cremini)
    mushrooms, roughly
    chopped
rapeseed (canola) oil for
    frying
approx. ½ tsp liquid
    smoke
salt

To serve

lingonberry jam

I like to serve this comfort food classic with a topping made from caramelised onion and chestnut (cremini) mushrooms flavoured with liquid smoke. The inspiration comes from the equally classic topping of fried bacon.

— First, make the topping. Fry the onions and mushrooms in oil until they've coloured nicely and the onions are soft. Add a dash of liquid smoke and a little salt. Stir, taste and season with more salt and liquid smoke if needed.
— For the pancakes, mix the potatoes together with the flour, salt, baking powder and milk and whisk to make a batter. Fry one pancake (100–150ml/3½–5fl oz/about ½ cup of batter) at a time in oil until golden brown on both sides.
— Serve the freshly fried pancakes topped with the mushrooms and onions, and some lingonberry jam.

51

HASH BROWNS

Serves 4 as a starter

6 large, firm potatoes
rapeseed (canola) oil for
    frying
salt and black pepper

Caviar sauce

3 tbsp unsweetened soya
    milk without added
    calcium
100ml/3½fl oz/scant ½
    cup rapeseed (canola)
    oil
1 tsp Dijon mustard or
    Skånsk mustard
1–2 tsp lemon juice
1 small red onion, finely
    chopped
6–7 tbsp chopped fresh
    dill – reserve a few
    sprigs to garnish
50g/1¾oz vegan caviar
    (seaweed pearls)

To serve

1 lemon, cut into wedges

Pickled mushrooms

250g/9oz firm mushrooms,
    preferably chestnut
    (cremini) mushrooms
2 tbsp distilled vinegar
    (24%) or 4 tbsp
    distilled vinegar (12%)
    or 120ml/4fl oz/½ cup
    distilled vinegar (5–6%)
1 tsp salt

Hash browns are so easy to make: all you need is potatoes, salt and pepper! The vegan caviar sauce is also good as a sandwich filling and if you want to make it more substantial you can crumble in some tofu. I often add pickled mushrooms to the sauce (instead of the traditional pickled herring) and serve for Easter, Midsummer and Christmas – delicious!

— First, make the sauce. Put the soya milk, rapeseed oil, mustard and lemon juice in a bowl and blend to make a thick mayonnaise, using a stick blender.
— Stir half of the onion into the mayonnaise (serve the rest in a bowl on the side). Stir in the dill and seaweed caviar and season to taste with salt and pepper. If you have any seaweed caviar left over you can serve this on the side.
— Peel the potatoes and grate using the fine side of the grater, onto a clean cloth. Squeeze out as much liquid as you can from the potato and place it in a bowl. Add salt and pepper. Divide the grated potato into four equal portions.
— Heat a little oil in a frying pan (skillet) and add one portion of the potato. Spread it out using a fork and fry until golden brown on one side. Flip over and fry on the other side. Repeat with the remaining potato.
— Serve the hash browns with the caviar sauce, lemon wedges and any remaining dill sprigs, red onion and seaweed caviar.

Pickled mushrooms

— Cut the mushrooms into bite-sized chunks. Bring 300ml/10fl oz/1¼ cups water to the boil in a pan together with the distilled vinegar and salt and add the mushrooms.
— Remove from the heat and leave the mushrooms in the brine until completely cooled. Drain the mushrooms and mix with the caviar sauce before serving.

WAFFLE TOASTIES WITH CREAMED MUSHROOMS

Makes 2

4 slices of bread
fresh herbs, e.g. basil or
  parsley

Creamed mushrooms

olive oil
1 shallot, finely chopped
8 chestnut (cremini)
  mushrooms, sliced
1 garlic clove, crushed
100ml/3½fl oz/scant ½
  cup oat cream,
  preferably home-made
  (see page 46)
1 tsp Dijon mustard
½ tbsp light soy sauce
½ tsp dried thyme
salt and black pepper

At a guess, I make waffles about twice a year; the rest of the time my waffle iron just sits in the cupboard. That is, until I realised I could use it for making waffle toasties, and now it's working a bit harder. The creamed mushrooms can be made in a big batch in advance and kept in the fridge. Then it will only take a couple of minutes to make a toastie once hunger kicks in.

— For the creamed mushrooms, heat a little olive oil in a frying pan (skillet) and fry the shallot and mushrooms until the mushrooms have coloured nicely. Season with salt and pepper. Add the garlic and oat cream and stir in the mustard, soy sauce and thyme. Leave to simmer for a minute and then remove from the heat.
— Drizzle olive oil over one side of each slice of bread. Add a dollop of creamed mushrooms on two slices of bread (on the side without oil) and add a couple of leaves of basil or parsley. Place the second bread slice on top with the oiled side facing out and press it all together in a hot waffle iron. After about 1 minute the toastie should be golden brown and ready to serve. Repeat with the second toastie.

57

OKONOMIYAKI

—

Makes 2 large pancakes

100g/3½oz/1 cup gram
(chickpea/garbanzo)
flour
50g/1¾oz/scant ½ cup
plain (all-purpose) flour
2 tbsp tamari
1 tbsp baking powder
½ tsp salt
200–250g/7–9oz/3–3½
cups finely shredded
white cabbage
200–250g/7–9oz/1¾ cups
chopped leek
1 tbsp grated fresh ginger
(optional)
rapeseed (canola) oil for
frying

To serve

mayonnaise (see page 45)
or sesame sauce (see
page 148)
sriracha or other chilli
sauce
hoisin sauce (optional)
1–2 red chillies, sliced
(optional)
toasted sesame seeds
(optional)
fresh coriander (cilantro)

Okonomiyaki is a kind of Japanese pancake that can be varied depending on what ingredients you've got at home. In early summer before the white cabbage is ready to harvest I have a lot of pak choi and use that instead. I've also made it using chard. It's also nice to add some finely shredded carrot.

— Whisk together the chickpea flour, plain flour, 200ml/ 7fl oz/generous ¾ cup water, tamari, baking powder and salt. Stir in the cabbage, leek and ginger.
— Heat a frying pan (skillet) and add enough oil to just cover the base. Pour in half of the batter and spread out across the pan, using a spatula.
— Fry the okonomiyaki over a low–medium heat until it is golden brown. Place an upside-down plate over the frying pan (the plate should be as large as or larger than the pan). Hold the plate steady and flip the pan upside down to turn the cabbage pancake out onto the plate (be careful if there's a lot of oil in the pan). Then slide the pancake back into the pan and fry on the other side until golden. Repeat using the remaining batter.
— To serve, spoon over some mayo or sesame sauce and drizzle with chilli sauce. If using, drizzle with hoisin sauce, scatter over some red chillies and sprinkle with sesame seeds and coriander.

POTATO TORTILLA

—

Serves 2

100g/3½oz/1 cup gram (chickpea/garbanzo) flour
1 tsp baking powder
1 tsp apple cider vinegar
rapeseed (canola) oil for frying
3 small brown onions, sliced
3 large garlic cloves, sliced
1 red chilli, finely chopped
1 tsp dried rosemary
4 potatoes, peeled and thinly sliced
salt

To serve

lemon juice
rocket (arugula)
sambal oelek

This simple but flavourful dish is one of my favourites and I go through periods when I eat it at least once a week. I've always got the ingredients at home and the flavour is hearty, herby and delicious. This is proper comfort food!

— Whisk together the flour, baking powder, 250ml/9fl oz/1 cup water, vinegar and 1 teaspoon salt to make a smooth batter.
— Heat a little oil in a frying pan (skillet) and fry the onions, garlic, chilli and rosemary for a couple of minutes until the onion starts to soften.
— Add the potatoes to the frying pan and fry until the potato starts to feel soft. Sprinkle with salt. Tip the onion and potato mixture into the batter, making sure you scrape the frying pan clean.
— Pour a little more oil into the frying pan and turn the heat down to low–medium. Pour the batter into the pan and even it out using a spatula. Cover with a lid and fry the tortilla for 10 minutes or until the surface has started to set.
— Place an upside-down plate over the frying pan (the plate should be as large as or larger than the pan). Hold the plate steady and flip the pan upside down to turn the tortilla out onto the plate. Then slide the tortilla back into the pan and fry on the other side until it has a golden brown surface.
— To serve, drizzle a little lemon juice over the rocket. Slice the tortilla into wedges and serve with the rocket and sambal oelek.

KOREAN PANCAKES

—

Makes 4–6 wedges

150g/5½oz/1¼ cups plain (all-purpose) flour
2 tbsp cornflour (cornstarch)
3 tbsp rapeseed (canola) oil, plus extra for frying
2 tbsp white miso paste
150g/5½oz/1 cup finely chopped leek
75g/2½oz/scant ½ cup sauerkraut or kimchi (optional)

Dipping sauce

1 small shallot, finely chopped
⅓ chilli, chopped
3 tbsp tamari
1 tbsp lemon juice
1 tsp sesame oil
1 tsp sesame seeds

These pancakes are similar to okonomiyaki (see page 61) but are a lot thinner. Traditionally they're eaten cut into wedges and served with a dipping sauce, but I also like to serve them as a wrap or crepe filled with, for example, finely shredded red cabbage and carrot, fried tofu, chilli mayo, sriracha sauce and fresh coriander (cilantro) or other things I've got at home. That way this becomes more like a filling dinner rather than a lunch dish. Pictured here are pancakes served with the dipping sauce, finely sliced chilli, white and black sesame seeds and lime wedges.

— Mix together the plain flour and cornflour in a bowl, then whisk in the rapeseed oil, miso paste and 400ml/14fl oz/ 1⅔ cups water to make a lump-free batter. Stir in the leek and, if using, the sauerkraut or kimchi. Leave to rest for 5 minutes.
— Mix all the ingredients for the dipping sauce together in a small bowl and set aside.
— Heat up a frying pan (skillet), pour in a thin layer of oil and then pour in enough batter to cover the whole pan, slightly thicker than a standard pancake (crepe). Fry over a medium heat until the surface has set, then flip over with a spatula and fry the other side until it is golden brown. Repeat with the remaining batter.
— Cut the pancakes into wedges and serve with the dipping sauce on the side.

SCRAMBLED TOFU

—

Serves 4

½ brown onion, finely
   chopped
vegetable oil for frying
1 pack plain tofu
   (250g/9oz), crumbled
1 tbsp nutritional yeast
pinch of ground turmeric
3–6 tbsp unsweetened
   oat or soya milk
salt and black pepper

To serve

1 spring onion (scallion),
   finely sliced
chilli flakes (optional)
good bread

If you want an extra filling breakfast or brunch, this quick little dish is wonderful with crispbread or toast. It's also good served with rocket (arugula), sliced avocado or slow-roasted tomatoes.

— Gently fry the onion in oil with a little salt and pepper until softened.
— Add the tofu to the pan and fry for 5–10 minutes. When the onion and tofu start to turn golden, add the nutritional yeast, turmeric and oat milk (add enough to get the consistency you like). Leave to simmer for 1 minute and then add salt and pepper to taste.
— Sprinkle the scrambled tofu with spring onion and chilli flakes if you like, and serve with bread.

PAELLA

—

Serves 4

100ml/3½fl oz/scant ½
  cup olive oil
2 brown onions, thinly
  sliced
2 peppers, preferably one
  yellow and one red,
  deseeded and chopped
  into chunks
pinch of saffron
1 tsp cayenne pepper
1 tbsp paprika
500g/1lb 2oz cherry or
  plum tomatoes, halved
300g/11oz/1⅔ cups long
  grain rice
200g/7oz green beans,
  trimmed
400g/14oz can
  cannellini or other large
  white beans, drained,
  or 250g/9oz/1⅓ cups
  cooked white beans
60g/2oz/scant ½ cup
  olives
1 large handful fresh
  flat-leaf parsley,
  roughly chopped
salt and black pepper

This dish is great when you have a lot of people to feed, as long as you have a large enough pan to cook the paella in. In the summer and autumn I like to cook it outside in a campfire skillet, which adds another dimension, with a lightly barbecued flavour.

— Heat the oil in a large frying pan (skillet) and gently fry the onions and peppers until the onion has softened. Add the spices, season with salt and pepper and fry for 1 minute. Add the tomatoes, rice and 600ml/1 pint/2½ cups water, cover and leave to simmer until the rice is cooked through, 15–20 minutes. You may need to add up to 200ml/7fl oz/ generous ¾ cup boiling water if the rice absorbs all the water before it is cooked.
— When there's around 5 minutes of the cooking time remaining, add the green and white beans. Taste and season with more salt and pepper if needed. Top with the olives and parsley and serve.

69

VEGETABLE FRITTERS

—

Serves 4

Carrot fritters

200g/7oz carrots, peeled
    and finely grated
1 large brown onion, finely
    chopped
1 garlic clove, grated
75g/2½oz/generous ¾
    cup gram (chickpea/
    garbanzo) flour
2 tsp baking powder

Beetroot fritters

120g/4oz beetroot
    (beets), peeled and
    finely grated
2 large brown onions,
    finely chopped
75–100g/2½–3½oz/¾–1
    cup gram (chickpea/
    garbanzo) flour
2 tsp baking powder
1 tsp dried rosemary

Courgette fritters

300g/11oz courgettes
    (zucchini), coarsely
    grated
1 large brown onion, finely
    chopped
1 garlic clove, grated
75g/2½oz/generous ¾
    cup gram (chickpea/
    garbanzo) flour
2 tsp baking powder

salt and black pepper
rapeseed (canola) oil for
    frying

These fritters are ridiculously simple, quick to make and can be varied according to what vegetables you've got at home or fancy eating. In the summer I use courgettes (zucchini); in the autumn and winter I use root vegetables such as carrot or beetroot (beets) and spice them up using umami-packed herbs or a tablespoon of grated ginger.

Chickpea flour really comes into its own here: it adds protein to the fritters and gives them a fluffy, light texture; a far cry from mushy bean patties.

— If you are using courgettes, sprinkle the grated courgette with salt and leave on the chopping board for a few minutes to draw out some of the liquid. Using your hands or a clean cloth, squeeze out as much liquid as possible.
— Place all the ingredients in a bowl, season generously with salt and black pepper and stir until thoroughly mixed. Shape into patties and fry in oil over a medium heat until the fritters have a nice colour on both sides. Serve hot.

FENNEL PASTA

___

Serves 4

2 fennel bulbs
100ml/3½fl oz/scant ½
   cup olive oil
5 garlic cloves, crushed
60g/2oz/scant ½ cup
   unsalted cashew nuts
250g/9oz spaghetti
1 tbsp nutritional yeast
salt and black pepper

To serve

freshly grated lemon zest
   (optional)
rocket (arugula)

The Italian kitchen is a great go-to when cooking plant-based food. Here, the focus is on a few carefully chosen ingredients and flavour buddies, making the food both simple and elegant. For this pasta dish I use fennel but it tastes just as good with courgettes (zucchini), cavolo nero or chard.

— Cut the fennel in half and trim off the root end, then cut into thin slices.
— Heat a frying pan (skillet) and add the olive oil, fennel and garlic. Add salt and pepper, cover with a lid and leave to cook on a low–medium heat for about 20 minutes or until the fennel is very soft. Stir occasionally to make sure it doesn't burn.
— Meanwhile, blend the cashew nuts to make a coarse flour and set aside.
— Boil the spaghetti; remove it from the heat when it still has a few minutes left to cook. Drain in a colander, keeping some of the water. Add the spaghetti to the fennel and ladle in the pasta water, starting with 4–5 tablespoons and adding more if needed, as the pasta absorbs the water.
— Add the cashew nuts, nutritional yeast and more pasta water until you've got a creamy sauce. Season to taste with salt and pepper and serve as soon as the pasta is cooked through. If you like, grate over some lemon zest and serve with rocket.

PANKO TEMPURA

📷 page 74

Serves 3–4 as a snack

1 pack plain tofu (250g/9oz),
    1 courgette (zucchini) or
    2 avocados
rapeseed (canola) oil or
    coconut oil for deep
    frying
about 100g/3½oz/2 cups
    panko breadcrumbs

Tempura batter

80g/2¾oz/⅔ cup plain
    (all-purpose) flour
2 tbsp baking powder
1 tsp caster (superfine)
    sugar
pinch of salt
1 tbsp vegetable oil
125ml/white4fl oz/½ cup
    sparkling water (you
    can also use tap water)

Crispy deep-fried food is great as a snack, starter or as a part of a main course. Deep-fried tofu is perfect as a replacement for battered fish, with chips or mashed potatoes, boiled peas and a cold dill sauce. The deep-fried avocado makes a nice snack to go with drinks as a part of a buffet, and the courgette (zucchini) is great served with a hearty salad.

— First, make the tempura batter: mix the dry ingredients together in a bowl, add the oil and water and whisk together. Leave to stand in a cool place for 10–15 minutes.
— Cut the tofu, courgette or avocados into bite-sized chunks.
— Add a few centimetres of oil to a deep pan. Heat the oil to 180°C/350°F – it is best to check using a thermometer. If you don't have a thermometer, add a small piece of bread to the oil: it should turn golden brown after about 1 minute.
— Dip a few chunks of tofu or vegetables into the tempura batter and let any excess batter drip off for a few seconds, then roll them in the panko and lower them into the hot oil. It should start to sizzle immediately, if it doesn't, the oil isn't hot enough. Deep-fry a few chunks at a time and leave to drain on a piece of kitchen paper while you fry the rest. Serve hot.

OPEN SANDWICH WITH FRIED EDAMAME

📷 page 75

Makes 4

250g/9oz/1⅔ cups
    edamame (green
    soybeans) or fresh
    broad (fava) beans
olive oil for frying
2 shallots, finely chopped
2 garlic cloves, thinly
    sliced
pinch of chilli flakes
4 slices of sourdough
    bread
1 batch lemon mayo (see
    page 45)
2 handfuls rocket
    (arugula)
lemon zest (optional)
salt and black pepper

When we have overnight guests I like to serve up a satisfying breakfast and this open sandwich with lemon mayonnaise and fried edamame beans is fresh, hearty and quick to rustle up. The beans make it filling enough to last you until lunch.

— If you are using broad beans, boil them in salted water for about a minute, then remove the pale, tough skins.
— Heat a little olive oil in a frying pan (skillet) and fry the shallots, garlic and beans over a low–medium heat until the beans have softened and warmed through. Add chilli flakes, salt and pepper to taste.
— Spread the bread with mayonnaise, add the rocket and top with the fried beans. Grate lemon zest over, if using.

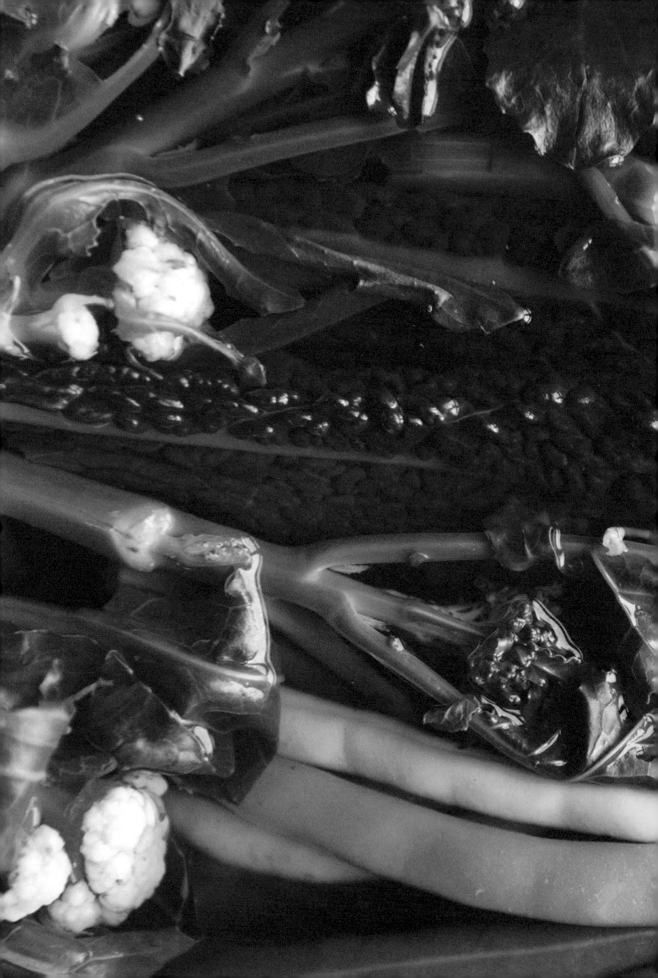

IV

IN
THE POT

ROASTED SWEETCORN SOUP

—

Serves 4

600g/1lb 5oz squash,
e.g. butternut or onion
squash (Hokkaido/red
kuri/small red hubbard
squash)
2 brown onions (approx.
200g/7oz), cut into
chunks
2 tbsp vegetable oil for
the roasting pan
500g/1lb 2oz/4 cups
frozen sweetcorn
1 small garlic bulb, sliced
horizontally
2 large handfuls fresh
coriander (cilantro)
½ tsp crushed coriander
seeds
2 mild chillies or 1
hotter, or to taste,
roughly chopped
salt and black pepper
toasted sunflower seeds
and/or sesame seeds,
to garnish (optional)

The best way to cook really umami-packed and
filling vegetable soups is to roast the ingredients in
the oven first, giving them a browned surface and
bringing out the sweet flavours. Here I use sweetcorn, squash and onion but you could also use,
for example, cauliflower, sweet potato, beetroots
(beets), carrots or Jerusalem artichokes.

— Preheat the oven to 250°C/500°F/Gas 9.
— Scrub the squash with a vegetable brush. Cut it in half,
remove the seeds and then cut the flesh into chunks: you
should have about 500g/1lb 2oz. Put the onions in an oiled
roasting pan together with the squash, sweetcorn and the
halved garlic bulb. Roast in the middle of the oven for 30
minutes or until the vegetables have started to brown and
the squash has softened.
— Transfer the roasted vegetables to a large pan; if you like, set
aside a handful of sweetcorn to garnish the finished soup.
Cut off the coriander leaves and place the stalks in the pan,
along with the coriander seeds, chilli and 1 litre/1¾ pints/
4 cups water. Using a stick blender, blend until smooth.
— To serve, add salt and pepper to taste and bring to the boil.
Serve the soup in bowls, topped with the coriander leaves
and reserved sweetcorn. It's also nice with toasted sunflower
seeds and sesame seeds, with some good bread on the side.

COLCANNON

—

Serves 4

1kg/2¼lb floury potatoes, peeled and cut into chunks

75g/2½oz/5 tbsp dairy-free spread, plus extra for frying and topping

approx. 150ml/5fl oz/ ⅔ cup unsweetened oat milk

200–250g/7–9oz/1¾ cups chopped leek

350g/12oz/4 cups chopped white cabbage

salt and black pepper

This Irish cabbage and potato mash is delicious as a side dish, but on nights when all I want is to devour comfort food on the sofa, it's not unheard of for me to eat this on its own, with a spoonful of lingonberry jam. It's also good with fried mushrooms to serve alongside.

— Boil the potatoes in salted water until thoroughly soft. Drain, then mash the potatoes using a potato masher, add the spread and oat milk and stir together to make a smooth mash. Add salt and pepper to taste.

— While the potatoes are boiling, gently fry the leek and cabbage in dairy-free spread until they have softened but without letting them colour.

— Fold the cabbage mixture into the mash. Pile into a bowl, make a little dip in the middle, add a dollop of dairy-free spread and leave to melt. To finish off, crack some pepper over the mash.

PASTA WITH CREAMY AVOCADO SAUCE

—

Serves 2

200g/7oz pasta
2 avocados
6 tbsp chopped fresh
  parsley
grated zest of 1 lemon,
  plus 1 tbsp juice
2 tbsp olive oil
2 tbsp nutritional yeast
1 garlic clove
½ chilli or a few pinches of
  chilli flakes
3–4 tbsp flaked almonds
salt and black pepper

This is real fast food: while the pasta boils you blend the avocado sauce and you have a gorgeous, filling lunch or dinner in no time at all. The toasted almonds bring a bit of luxury to the dish while adding both crunchiness and a nutty flavour. This is good served with fresh spinach and rocket (arugula).

— Boil the pasta according to the instructions on the pack.
— Halve the avocados, remove the stones and scoop the flesh into a bowl. Add the parsley, lemon juice, olive oil, nutritional yeast, garlic and chilli, and season with salt and pepper. Blend together then taste and add more salt and pepper if needed.
— Toast the flaked almonds in a dry frying pan (skillet) until they're golden brown.
— Drain the pasta and stir the pasta together with the avocado sauce. Divide between two bowls, sprinkle over the lemon zest and finish by scattering over the flaked almonds.

RICE BOWL WITH STEAMED VEGETABLES AND PEANUT SAUCE

—

Serves 4

Rice bowl

225–300g/8–11oz/
   approx. 1½ cups rice
1 pack plain tofu (250g/
   9oz), cut into chunks
vegetable oil for frying
1 tbsp tamari
1–2 handfuls fresh
   coriander (cilantro)
salt and black pepper

Vegetables, such as:

2 carrots
1 head of broccoli or small
   cauliflower
1 large handful green
   beans
1 handful mangetout
   (snow peas)
1 handful small cavolo
   nero leaves
1 large handful rocket
   (arugula) or baby
   spinach

Peanut sauce

2 shallots, chopped
vegetable oil for frying
2 tsp red curry paste
240g/8½oz/1⅔ cups
   roasted and salted
   peanuts, plus extra for
   topping (optional)
4cm/1½in chunk of fresh
   ginger, grated
2 garlic cloves, grated
2 tbsp tamari

Unlike most other recipes in this book, this one involves several different steps and uses almost all the cooking plates on the hob. But it's not an especially complicated dish and it's a weekday favourite all year round at my place. It's really versatile and you can use whatever vegetables you've got at home or whatever you like.

— Boil the rice according to the instructions on the pack.
— Prepare the vegetables: cut any large vegetables into chunks; cut broccoli or cauliflower into florets; trim other veg as necessary. Steam the vegetables (not rocket or baby spinach) until they feel tender.
— Season the tofu with salt and pepper and fry in oil, turning until golden brown on all sides. Pour over the tamari and shake the pan to coat the tofu.
— To make the peanut sauce, fry the shallots in oil until softened. Add the curry paste and fry for about a minute. Blend the peanuts with 400ml/14fl oz/1⅔ cups water and pour into the pan. Add the ginger, garlic and tamari. Simmer for about a minute or until the sauce starts to thicken, then remove from the heat.
— To serve, divide the rice, vegetables and tofu among four bowls and top with the peanut sauce, coriander and chopped peanuts, if using.

87

LAKSA

📷 page 89

Serves 4

vegetable oil
2 tsp red curry paste
1½ tbsp grated fresh
    ginger
3 garlic cloves, grated
3 Kaffir lime leaves
400ml/14fl oz can
    coconut cream
1 tsp bouillon powder (see
    page 40) or 1 vegetable
    stock cube
2 tbsp tamari
250g/9oz tofu or field
    mushrooms
salt

Toppings

250g/9oz/1⅓ cup beans,
    e.g. edamame (green
    soybeans) or cooked
    black beans
2 handfuls green beans or
    mangetout (snow peas)
250g/9oz wheat, rice or
    glass noodles
2 large spring onions
    (scallions), sliced
pea shoots or fresh
    spinach
fresh coriander (cilantro)
1 lemon or lime, halved

Laksa is a quick-to-make noodle soup from South East Asia that is similar to ramen, but is made from a coconut-based broth instead. As with ramen, you can choose toppings depending on what you like, have at home or what's in season. I like to have around half of the toppings cooked while keeping the rest raw and crisp.

If you want to speed up the process and skip the step of frying tofu, you can instead use mushrooms that you cook in the broth.

— Heat a little oil in a large pan. Add the curry paste, ginger, garlic and lime leaves and fry for a few minutes. Add the coconut cream, 700ml/24fl oz/3 cups water, bouillon powder and tamari. Bring to the boil and season to taste with salt. If you are using mushrooms, clean them and cut into wedges, then simmer them in the broth for a few minutes.
— Bring water to the boil in another pan and boil any toppings that need cooking. Edamame and green beans take around 5–8 minutes while the cooking time for the noodles can vary; if you're using noodles that only need about a minute, add these towards the end. Strain and rinse the vegetables and noodles in cold water and leave to drain.
— If you are using tofu, cut it into cubes and fry in oil, turning until golden brown on all sides, adding salt towards the end.
— Divide the noodles and beans among four serving bowls. Ladle over the broth and top with the tofu, sliced spring onions, pea shoots or spinach, and coriander. Squeeze over some lemon or lime juice and serve immediately.

ROSEHIP SOUP

📷 page 93

**Makes approx. 1 litre/
1¾ pints/4 cups**

400ml/14fl oz/1⅔ cups
    dried or fresh
    rosehips, ends trimmed
85g/3oz/scant ½ cup
    granulated sugar, plus
    extra to taste
1 tbsp vanilla sugar

In the autumn I get out early and pick lots of rose-hips that I dry and then use for making rosehip soup whenever I wish. When I was a child I refused to eat gruel and was instead fed warm rosehip soup, and I still love it. The soup is nice to drink straight from the fridge, or warmed up and topped with a generous dollop of whipped soya cream and a little vanilla sugar and cinnamon sprinkled on top.

It's easy to dry rosehips: trim off the ends and place on a baking sheet lined with baking parch-ment. Dry in the oven at its lowest setting (approx. 70°C/160°F) until they're completely dry but don't let them catch any colour. To avoid running the oven for several hours I usually leave them to dry in the residual heat after I've used the oven for something else. After that they can continue to dry at room temperature and then get another round in residual heat the following day.

— Put the rosehips in a pan, add 1 litre/1¾ pints/4 cups water, bring to the boil and boil for 15 minutes, or until the rose-hips feel soft.
— Blend to make a grainy soup and then strain through a fine mesh sieve. Once you have strained the soup you can add 100–200ml/3½–7fl oz/about ½–¾ cup water to the sieve to wash out the last bit of soup from the pulp.
— Pour the soup into a clean pan, add the sugar and vanilla sugar and heat, stirring occasionally, until the sugar has dissolved. Taste and add more sugar if needed.

93

DAAL

📷 page 98

The very first thing I start to crave when the nights begin to get a little darker and cooler in August or September is a spicy daal. If you want to vary this a little you can replace the sweet potato with carrots, squash or cauliflower. If you want to add even more protein you can stir in some cooked chickpeas (garbanzos) or yellow peas. I usually serve this with rice cooked with cavolo nero.

— Heat a little oil in a pot and gently fry the onions and chillies together with a little salt until the onion is soft and has started to colour.

— Stir in the masala spices and fry for another minute. When it starts to catch at the bottom of the pot, add the sweet potato, chopped tomatoes, stock, lentils, lime leaves, garlic and ginger. Leave to simmer for 15–20 minutes or until the sweet potato is cooked through.

— Meanwhile, trim off any tough stalks from the cavolo nero and tear the leaves into pieces. Place them in a pan together with the rice, some salt and plenty of water. Cover and simmer until the rice is soft, then drain through a sieve.

— Add the coconut milk and lemon juice to the pot of daal and bring to the boil. Remove from the heat and season to taste with salt.

— Serve the daal together with the cavolo nero and rice and preferably some fresh coriander (cilantro) and cherry tomatoes, halved or quartered, depending on size.

Serves 4

vegetable oil
2 brown onions, sliced
2 red chillies, finely chopped
1½ tbsp masala (see below)
1 large sweet potato (approx. 600g/1lb 5oz), peeled and cut into bite-sized chunks
400g/14oz can chopped tomatoes
500ml/17fl oz/2 cups vegetable stock
170g/6oz/generous ¾ cup dried red lentils
3 dried Kaffir lime leaves (optional)
2 garlic cloves, grated
1½ tbsp grated fresh ginger
400ml/14fl oz can coconut milk
1 tbsp lemon juice
salt

Masala

1 tbsp ground cumin
1 tbsp ground cinnamon
1 tbsp ground ginger
2 tsp ground turmeric
2 tsp cayenne pepper

To serve

5 cavolo nero leaves
225g/8oz/1¼ cups rice

94

MY BEST TOMATO SOUP

📷 page 99

Serves 3–4

2 brown onions, finely
   sliced
2 carrots, sliced
2 celery stalks, sliced
2 chillies, finely chopped
1 tbsp finely chopped
   fresh sage
vegetable oil
1 tsp ground caraway (or
   crushed caraway seeds)
1 tsp dried thyme
1 tsp dried rosemary
500g/1lb 2oz passata or
   chopped tomatoes
3½ tbsp tamari
4 garlic cloves, grated
85–100g/3–3½oz large
   macaroni or other pasta
salt and black pepper

The first time I made this soup I set out to make something hearty, savoury, warming and filling – in other words, a proper vegan comfort dish. I maxed the flavours by adding herbs, chilli, tamari, celery and lots of onion and garlic.

The result was so heartwarmingly delicious that I couldn't stop eating. Over and over again I returned to the kitchen with my soup bowl until I had finished almost the whole batch! I fell into such a food coma that I fell asleep on the sofa and didn't wake up for several hours – and I was still lovely and warm from the inside out. Yes, this is my best ever tomato soup!

— Fry the onions, carrots, celery, chillies and sage in oil with salt and pepper until the onion has softened and started to get a bit of colour. Add the caraway and herbs and fry for a few more minutes.
— Stir in the passata, tamari and garlic, add about 600ml/ 1 pint/2½ cups water, bring to the boil and simmer for 10–15 minutes.
— Add the pasta and leave the soup to simmer until the pasta is soft. Serve immediately.

WHITE BEAN DIP

—

Serves 4

400g/14oz can white
  beans, drained, or
  250g/9oz/1⅓ cups
  cooked white beans
3½ tbsp olive oil
1½ tsp lemon juice
½ tsp sesame oil
1 small garlic clove,
  peeled
salt and black pepper

Extra flavourings (optional)

fresh dill, artichokes in oil
  or sun-dried tomatoes
  and fresh basil

This is a really versatile dish that can be used in many ways. As a spread on crispbread or sourdough bread, as a side dish with roasted vegetables or salad, or dolloped onto wraps, salads or almost anything you can think of.

I recommend trying it with preserved grilled artichokes in oil on a slice of bread. When I was holidaying for a few days in the Faroe Islands I ate this a couple of times every day as it was difficult to get hold of plant-based food. After a whole loaf of rye bread I still hadn't got fed up with this delicious flavour combination.

— Put the beans, olive oil, lemon juice, sesame oil and garlic in a blender or food processor and blend until smooth. Season to taste with salt and pepper. (You may also want to add a little more sesame oil to taste.)
— If you'd like to add dill, artichokes or tomato and basil to the dip, add them along with the other ingredients before blending – setting aside a little dill or basil to garnish.

CHILLI

—

Gather round the campfire: here is a recipe for a real bang-bang chilli! This hot and hearty stew can be made in a jiffy or left to slow cook. Or you can make it a day in advance – it will just get more and more delicious. Serve with sourdough bread and maybe some nachos for dipping.

Serves 4

2 brown onions, sliced
2 red (bell) peppers, deseeded and roughly chopped
2 chillies, or to taste, finely chopped
vegetable oil for frying
1 tbsp paprika
1½ tsp ground cumin
3 bay leaves
3 garlic cloves, grated
400g/14oz can chopped tomatoes
170g/6oz/generous ¾ cup dried red lentils
3 tbsp tamari or Japanese soy sauce
600g/1lb 5oz cooked kidney beans and white beans
100g/3½oz/generous ¾ cup frozen sweetcorn
salt and black pepper

— Fry the onions, peppers and chillies in oil until the onion has softened and started to colour.
— Add the spices, bay leaves and garlic and fry for another minute. Stir in the chopped tomatoes, 600ml/1 pint/ 2½ cups water, lentils and tamari and simmer for at least 15 minutes, but preferably longer.
— Add the beans and sweetcorn and simmer for another couple of minutes. Season to taste with salt and pepper.

Makes 10

Bao

15g/½oz fresh yeast
  (or 7g/¼oz dried)
300ml/10fl oz/1¼ cups
  tepid water
375g/13oz/3 cups plain
  (all-purpose) flour, plus
  extra for dusting
1 tbsp caster (superfine)
  sugar
1 tbsp rapeseed
  (canola) oil, plus extra
  for brushing
1 tsp salt

Pulled jackfruit

4 brown onions, thinly
  sliced
rapeseed (canola) oil
2 x 585g/1lb 4oz cans
  jackfruit in brine,
  drained
1½ tbsp paprika
1 tsp chilli powder
1 tsp dried thyme
2 x 400g/14oz cans
  chopped tomatoes
5 tbsp tamari
1 tbsp granulated sugar
4 garlic cloves
¾ tsp liquid smoke
salt and black pepper

PULLED JACKFRUIT BAOS

📷 page 106–107

Steaming bread dough gives it a special texture: fluffy, light and chewy. In this recipe the bao buns are folded in half in the traditional way, but to speed up the process you could roll the dough into balls, steam, and then slice them in half, like a burger bun. And if you'd like to quickly rustle up this dish on a weekday you can replace the bao with bread rolls, tortillas or focaccia.

Jackfruit is a tropical fruit with a texture that resembles slow-cooked meat. You will find canned jackfruit in Asian food stores and some supermarkets. It comes in either syrup or in brine: for this recipe you need the one in brine.

Bao
— Crumble the yeast into a bowl, add the water and stir until the yeast has dissolved. Add the remaining ingredients and work the dough for a few minutes in a stand mixer fitted with a dough hook. Cover the bowl with cling film (plastic wrap) or a damp tea (dish) towel and leave the dough to rise for 1 hour.
— On a floured work surface, roll out the dough into a long sausage and cut into ten pieces. Shape into round balls and then roll out into ovals, about 12 x 18cm/5 x 7in. Brush the tops with oil. Cut out 10cm/4in squares from the baking parchment. Fold the ovals in half, placing a square of baking parchment in between. Place the bao buns on baking parchment, cover with a dry tea (dish) towel and leave to prove for 1–1½ hours.

Coleslaw

200g/7oz white cabbage,
   finely shredded
½ small red onion, thinly
   sliced
1 batch mayonnaise (see
   page 45)

To serve

fresh coriander (cilantro)
sriracha sauce or other
   chilli sauce

— Bring water to the boil in a pan that fits your steamer. I use two bamboo baskets that stack on top of each other. Cut out circles of baking parchment and place each bao bun on a piece of parchment. Place 1–2 buns in each steaming basket and steam for 10 minutes. Remove the baskets from the steamer, take out the buns and repeat until they are all steamed. Be careful, the steam gets very hot! Leave to cool slightly or completely before serving.

Pulled jackfruit

— In a large pan, fry the onions in rapeseed oil with some salt and pepper until the onions are soft and golden.
— Add the jackfruit and fry for a few minutes. Stir in the paprika, chilli powder and thyme and fry for 1 minute. Add the chopped tomatoes, tamari and sugar and grate in the garlic. Cover the pan and leave to simmer for about 1 hour, stirring occasionally to make sure it doesn't catch at the bottom. I usually take the lid off for the last 15 minutes so the mixture can reduce and thicken.
— Crush the jackfruit with a wooden spoon. Add the liquid smoke, then taste and add more seasoning if needed.

Coleslaw

— In a bowl, mix together the cabbage, onion and mayonnaise. Season to taste with salt and pepper.

— To serve, fill the bao buns with the pulled jackfruit and top with coleslaw, coriander and sriracha or other chilli sauce.

NOODLE BROTH WITH OYSTER MUSHROOMS

—

Serves 2

100g/3½oz oyster
   mushrooms
1 brown onion or 2
   shallots, sliced
vegetable oil
1 garlic clove, grated
1 tbsp grated fresh ginger
½ red chilli, chopped
2 tbsp tamari
100g/3½oz edamame
   (green soybeans)
1 handful mangetout
   (snow peas)
150g/5½oz wheat or rice
   noodles or 300g/11oz
   fresh udon noodles
1–2 spring onions
   (scallions), sliced
1 large handful fresh
   coriander (cilantro)
salt and Sichuan pepper

Of course you can make this with a different type of mushroom, but I do recommend trying oyster mushrooms at some point – they have become one of my absolute favourites. The slightly stringy texture means that the mushrooms almost resemble the meat on a chicken thigh but with a nice mild mushroom flavour.

The broth only takes around 10–15 minutes to prepare and if you want to make it more elegant you can strain the broth to remove the onion just before adding the beans, and take out the mushrooms to add back to the soup later. But I'm a fan of simplicity and think the onion works well as a soup ingredient so I like to leave it as it is.

— Clean the mushrooms and tear into pieces. Fry the mushrooms and onion in a little oil until the mushrooms have started to colour. Add the garlic, ginger and chilli and fry for another minute. Add 600ml/1 pint/2½ cups water, the tamari, edamame and mangetout and leave to simmer for 5 minutes. Add salt and Sichuan pepper to taste.
— Meanwhile, boil the noodles in a separate pan. Drain in a colander and rinse them in cold water.
— Divide the noodles between two serving bowls, ladle over the broth and top with spring onion and coriander.

113

SARDINIAN FENNEL AND CHICKPEA SOUP

—

Serves 4–6

1 large fennel bulb
(approx. 300g/11oz)
3 tbsp olive oil
1 brown onion, sliced
2 large garlic cloves,
crushed
6–7 tbsp chopped fresh
parsley
3 potatoes, peeled and
finely diced
350g/12oz plum tomatoes,
diced
350g/12oz/2 cups cooked
chickpeas (garbanzos)
100g/3½oz small pasta
shapes
salt and black pepper

We quite often have people over for dinner and when we do I love to serve simple but filling food that's been prepared in advance and just needs reheating. I like to serve this soup with a home-baked sourdough bread for dipping. It's usually so popular that all the talking stops completely and is replaced with a choir of slurping.

— Cut the fronds from the fennel and chop them finely. Cut the fennel in half and trim a thin slice off the base. Slice the fennel thinly.
— Heat the oil in a pan, add the onion, garlic and 3 tablespoons parsley. Cover with a lid and leave to sweat for a few minutes until the onion has started to colour, stirring occasionally.
— Add the fennel fronds, fennel and potatoes and fry, uncovered, for around 10 minutes. Add the tomatoes, chickpeas and 1 litre/1¾ pints/4 cups water, season with salt and pepper and leave to simmer for 10–15 minutes.
— Add the pasta and simmer until soft.
— Using a spoon, carefully crush the potato chunks, stir in the remaining parsley and serve.

RIBOLLITA

📷 page 118

Serves 4

2 tbsp olive oil

2 carrots, cut into chunks

1 brown onion, cut into chunks

2 celery stalks, cut into chunks

1½ tbsp chopped fresh sage

2 tsp dried rosemary

2 tsp dried thyme

10 cavolo nero or kale leaves

3 potatoes, peeled and cut into chunks

800ml/28fl oz/3⅓ cups vegetable stock or water

600g/1lb 5oz/3⅓ cups cooked white beans, plus approx. 200ml/ 7fl oz/generous ¾ cup cooking liquid or water

5 marinated sun-dried tomatoes

2 garlic cloves, peeled

1–2 tsp lemon juice

salt and black pepper

Ribollita is a hearty farmer's soup from Tuscany that warms and fills you up. What I think is clever is that blended beans are used to thicken the soup; this is something I've adopted when making other soups. It's a super easy way to add extra protein to your food and 'hide' beans for the sceptics, at the same time as making the soup extra thick.

— Heat the oil in a large pan, add the carrots, onion, celery, herbs, and some salt and pepper and gently fry until the onion is soft.

— Trim off any tough stalks from the cavolo nero or kale and shred the leaves. Add the shredded leaves and potatoes to the onions and fry for about a minute, then add the stock or water. Cover and leave to simmer for 1 hour.

— Stir half of the beans into the soup. Blend the remaining beans together with their cooking liquid or water, the sun-dried tomatoes and garlic. Add the bean purée to the soup, stir and bring to the boil. Add lemon juice, salt and pepper to taste and serve hot.

HARIRA

📷 page 121

Serves 4

olive oil
2 brown onions, thinly
   sliced
2 carrots, cut into chunks
pinch of saffron
½ tsp coriander seeds
1 tsp ground cumin
1 tsp ground cinnamon
2 large handfuls fresh
   coriander (cilantro) or
   parsley, leaves and
   stalks separated
2 x 400g/14oz cans
   chopped tomatoes
170g/6oz/generous ¾ cup
   dried Puy lentils
approx. 425g/15oz/2½
   cups cooked yellow
   peas or chickpeas
   (garbanzos), or 2 x
   400g/14oz cans
   chickpeas, drained
salt and black pepper

This Moroccan soup gets its lovely aromatic flavour from spices including saffron, cumin, cinnamon and coriander. It's very filling as it's based on both lentils and peas.

— Heat a little oil in a pot and gently fry the onions until they start to colour. Add the carrots. Crush the dry spices together using a pestle and mortar, stir into the pot and gently fry for another minute.

— Chop the coriander stalks finely and add to the pot together with the chopped tomatoes and 800ml/28fl oz/ 3⅓ cups water. Cover and leave to simmer gently for 30 minutes.

— Add the lentils and simmer for another 30 minutes. When there's 10 minutes of the cooking time remaining, add the cooked peas or chickpeas, with salt and pepper to taste.

— Coarsely chop the coriander or parsley leaves and use to garnish the soup.

IN
THE OVEN

BAKED POTATOES WITH CURRIED TOFU

—

Serves 4

12 potatoes
1 pack plain tofu
   (250g/9oz)
1 small red onion,
   chopped
1 small apple, finely
   chopped
1 batch mayonnaise (see
   page 45)
200ml/7fl oz oat fraîche
2 tbsp Skånsk mustard
   (optional)
1–1½ tbsp curry powder
1 tsp paprika
salt and black pepper
1–2 spring onions
   (scallions), chopped, to
   garnish

I love all dishes that involve eating potato skin, so of course baked potatoes, with their well-baked skins, are one of my favourite dishes. I prefer to use slightly larger standard potatoes rather than huge baking potatoes: they need less time in the oven, are cheaper, and I get to eat a bit more of that lovely skin.

Here I've served them with creamy curried tofu. The curried tofu is also perfect with bread for breakfast or as a filling in a baguette for picnics. You can replace the tofu with pickled mushrooms if you prefer (see page 54).

— Preheat the oven to 225°C/425°F/Gas 7. Scrub the potatoes, place in a baking dish and prick them with a thin skewer. Bake the potatoes for 45 minutes, or until they feel soft in the middle.
— Crumble the tofu into coarse chunks and set aside. Stir all the remaining ingredients together in a bowl until thoroughly mixed. Stir in the tofu and season to taste with salt and pepper. Garnish with a sprinkling of chopped spring onion.
— Split the potatoes in half and serve together with the curried tofu and, if you like, a nice salad.

127

DOUBLE-BAKED POTATOES

—

Makes 20

10 potatoes
200ml/7fl oz oat fraîche
2 tbsp rapeseed (canola)
    oil
120g/4oz/¾ cup finely
    chopped leeks
1 tsp lemon juice
salt and black pepper
fresh dill, to garnish
    (optional)

These double-baked potatoes make a tasty snack or are nice on a buffet table. They are easy to make if you've got potatoes left over after a baked potato dinner.

— Preheat the oven to 225°C/425°F/Gas 7. Scrub the potatoes, place in a baking dish and prick them with a thin skewer. Bake the potatoes for 40 minutes, or until they feel soft in the middle. Leave to cool slightly so they're easier to handle. Turn the oven down to 200°C/400°F/Gas 6.

— Halve the potatoes and scoop out the flesh into a bowl. Mash lightly and mix with the remaining ingredients. Season to taste with salt and pepper.

— Add the filling to the potato skins and bake for 20 minutes. Garnish with dill, if using.

SHEPHERD'S PIE

📷 **page 126**

This British classic is my other half's favourite and it's always popular for Sunday family dinner. Serve with a green salad with a squeeze of lemon juice.

— Boil the potatoes in a large pan of salted water, covered with a lid, for about 20 minutes, or until soft.
— For the lentil mince, fry the onions, carrots and mushrooms in a generous glug of olive oil until the onions have started to colour. Add some salt, the white pepper and the herbs.
— Add the tomato purée and fry, stirring, for another few minutes. Add 800ml/28fl oz/3⅓ cups water, the lentils, tamari and bouillon powder and stir well. Cover and leave to simmer until the lentils are almost cooked through.
— Sprinkle over the flour and whisk into the mince, preferably using a steel whisk to make sure you get rid of any lumps of flour. Add up to 200ml/7fl oz/generous ¾ cup water until you've reached a good consistency.
— Preheat the oven to 200°C/400°F/Gas 6.
— Drain the boiled potatoes and mash them using a potato masher. Stir in the spread and milk and mash together until smooth. Season to taste with salt and black pepper. Scoop the mince into a baking dish and top with the mash. Bake for 25 minutes, or until the mash is golden brown.

Serves 4–6

Mash

1.2kg/2lb 10oz potatoes, peeled and cut into chunks
75g/2½oz/5 tbsp dairy-free spread
approx. 150ml/5fl oz/ ⅔ cup plant milk
salt and black pepper

Lentil mince

3 brown onions, finely chopped
2 carrots, finely chopped
5 large field mushrooms, finely chopped
olive oil for frying
1 tsp white pepper
1 tbsp finely chopped fresh rosemary
2 tbsp finely chopped fresh sage
3 tbsp tomato purée (tomato paste)
120g/4oz/scant ⅔ cup dried red lentils
85g/3oz/scant ½ cup dried beluga lentils
3 tbsp tamari
1 tbsp bouillon powder (see page 40)
2 tbsp plain (all-purpose) flour

CAKE TWO WAYS

📷 page 132

Makes 8 slices

160g/5¾oz/1¼ cups
   sifted spelt flour or
   plain (all-purpose) flour
3 tbsp psyllium husk or
   2 tbsp potato flour
125g/4½oz/scant ⅔ cup
   caster (superfine) sugar
1 tbsp baking powder
grated zest of 1 lemon
1 tbsp poppy seeds
200ml/7fl oz/generous
   ¾ cup unsweetened oat
   or soya milk
5 tbsp rapeseed (canola)
   oil
120g/4oz/generous ¾
   cup blueberries, fresh or
   frozen

Makes 8 slices

160g/5¾oz/1¼ cups
   sifted spelt flour or
   plain (all-purpose) flour
3 tbsp psyllium husk or 2
   tbsp potato flour
125g/4½oz/scant ⅔ cup
   caster (superfine) sugar
1 tbsp baking powder
pinch of saffron
200ml/7fl oz/generous ¾
   cup unsweetened oat or
   soya milk
5 tbsp rapeseed (canola)
   oil
3 tbsp flaked almonds

I often bake a cake when we're expecting guests; these are a few of my favourites. As you can see, the cakes use the same batter as a base, but one is flavoured with saffron and the other with lemon, poppy seeds and blueberries. I've also made them with gooseberry and vanilla, pear and dried ginger, and apple, cardamom and cinnamon. In other words, the only limit is your imagination and what's in your cupboard.

Lemon and poppy seed cake with blueberries
— Preheat the oven to 200°C/400°F/Gas 6. Line a cake tin (16–18cm/6½–7in diameter) with baking parchment, or grease and flour.
— Mix the dry ingredients together in a bowl. Add the milk and oil and stir thoroughly. Finally, stir in the blueberries.
— Pour the batter into the prepared tin. Bake in the middle of the oven for 35 minutes, or until a thin skewer comes out clean when inserted into the middle of the cake.

Saffron cake with almonds
— Preheat the oven to 200°C/400°F/Gas 6. Line a cake tin (16–18cm/6½–7in diameter) with baking parchment, or grease and flour.
— Mix the dry ingredients, apart from the almonds, together in a bowl. Add the milk and oil and stir thoroughly.
— Pour the batter into the prepared tin and top with the flaked almonds. Bake in the middle of the oven for 35 minutes, or until a thin skewer comes out clean when inserted into the middle of the cake.

CHOCOLATE CAKE WITH COFFEE AND HAZELNUTS

📷 page 133

Makes 8 slices

65g/2¼oz/scant ½ cup
hazelnuts
125g/4½oz/ ½ cup
dairy-free spread
200g/7oz/1 cup caster
(superfine) sugar
100g/3½oz/generous ¾
cup plain (all-purpose)
flour
100ml/3½fl oz/scant ½
cup aquafaba (water
from canned or
home-cooked
chickpeas or white
beans)
35g/1¼oz/scant ½ cup
cocoa powder
2 tbsp ground coffee
pinch of salt

If I know in advance that I have guests coming for coffee, I like to make this delicious sticky chocolate cake and leave it to rest in the fridge for a couple of hours or overnight. The hazelnuts can be excluded if you prefer, or if you or a guest has a nut allergy, but they marry very well with the aromatic coffee flavour.

— Preheat the oven to 200°C/400°F/Gas 6. Line a small cake tin (approx 16cm/6½in diameter) with baking parchment.
— Toast the hazelnuts in a dry frying pan (skillet) over a low heat until they're golden brown. Chop them coarsely and discard as much of the skin as possible.
— Melt the dairy-free spread in a pan. Remove from the heat, add the sugar and stir. Add the flour, aquafaba, cocoa powder, coffee and salt and stir to make a smooth batter. Finally, stir in the hazelnuts, saving some to sprinkle on top of the cake if you wish.
— Pour the batter into the prepared tin and top with the reserved nuts. Bake for about 18 minutes: the surface should be set but the cake should wobble in the middle if you shake it. Leave to cool completely and preferably leave in the fridge for at least a couple of hours before serving.

CREAMED MUSHROOMS IN A POTATO CRUST

—

Serves 4

Potato crust

4 cold cooked medium
  potatoes
140g/5oz/generous ¾
  cup rice flour
100ml/3½fl oz/scant ½
  cup rapeseed (canola)
  oil
½ tsp salt

Creamed mushrooms

5 large cavolo nero leaves
2 shallots, chopped
vegetable oil for frying
300g/11oz mushrooms,
  e.g. chestnut (cremini)
  mushrooms or ceps,
  sliced
1 tsp dried thyme
2 tsp arrowroot or plain
  (all-purpose) flour
200ml/7fl oz oat fraîche
1 tbsp light soy sauce or
  tamari
1 tsp Dijon mustard
1 large garlic clove,
  grated
salt and black pepper

This gluten-free crust is made from rice flour and leftover potatoes, and gets a potato crisp-like flavour once it's baked (you can use freshly boiled potatoes too). Filled with glorious creamed mushrooms it becomes a firm autumn favourite. Several times when I've made this for dinner, it has ended with us asking ourselves: Shall we make it for dinner again tomorrow?

— Preheat the oven to 225°C/425°F/Gas 7.
— Crush the potatoes using a potato ricer, or grate them. Mix with the rice flour, oil and salt to form a dough. Press the dough out into a flan dish (approx. 22cm/8½in diameter). Bake for 30 minutes or until the crust is golden brown.
— Trim off any tough stalks from the cavolo nero and tear the leaves into pieces.
— Fry the shallots in oil until they start to soften and then add the mushrooms and thyme and a sprinkling of salt to encourage the mushrooms to release their liquid quickly. When the mushrooms have coloured nicely, add the cavolo nero and gently fry for about another minute. Sprinkle over the arrowroot and stir, then add the oat fraîche, soy sauce, Dijon mustard, garlic and pepper. Leave to simmer gently until thickened.
— Pour the creamed mushrooms into the crust and serve.

135

HERBY FOCACCIA

📷 page 136–137

Makes 1 focaccia

15g/½oz fresh yeast (or
   7g/¼oz dried)
425g/15oz/3⅓ cups plain
   (all-purpose) flour
½ tsp sea salt or
   Himalayan salt
fresh herbs e.g. thyme,
   sage, rosemary
1–2 tbsp olive oil
salt flakes

Baking a large batch of focaccia to keep in the freezer can be a saviour in many situations. I serve the bread with soups, stews and salads of course, but it's also great as burger buns, with sausages or as filled panini (see page 140).

I leave my focaccia to rise overnight; this way the dough will develop more flavour, and the crumb will be a little more moist and chewy while the crust will be slightly crispier.

— Stir the yeast into 350ml/12fl oz/scant 1½ cups cold water in a large bowl until dissolved. Stir in the flour and salt and quickly work into a dough. Cover the bowl with cling film (plastic wrap) or a damp tea (dish) towel and leave the dough to rise for 1 hour.
— Line a roasting pan (approx. 33 x 33cm/13 x 13in) with baking parchment and tip the dough into it. Rinse your hands with cold water and press the dough out evenly in the pan. Cover with cling film (plastic wrap) or a damp tea (dish) towel and leave in the fridge for about 12 hours or overnight.
— Preheat the oven to 225°C/425°F/Gas 7.
— Arrange the herb leaves on top of the dough, drizzle with oil and press your fingertips into the dough to create dips. Finish off with a sprinkling of salt flakes. Bake the focaccia in the middle of the oven for 20 minutes or until risen and golden brown.

FOCACCIA PANINI

—

Makes 4 large sandwiches

⅓ focaccia (see page 138)
50–70g/1¾–2½oz/scant
   ½ cup–⅔ cup grated
   plant-based cheese
4 good-quality sun-dried
   tomatoes in oil, cut into
   strips
15 fresh basil leaves
olive oil

If you have any focaccia leftover from dinner it's delicious to fill and warm in the waffle iron. Perfect for a weekend breakfast or a quick lunch.

— Cut the focaccia into four portion-sized pieces. Slice them in half and add cheese, tomatoes and basil onto one half. It's good to have cheese against both bread slices so that the sandwich is 'glued' together when warmed in the waffle iron. Place the second half of the bread on top.

— Heat a waffle iron and drizzle with a little oil. Place one sandwich in the waffle iron, drizzle with a little oil and then press it together. Grill for about a minute, until the panini is flat and has a nice golden colour. Repeat with the remaining sandwiches.

PARSNIP CAKE

———

Makes 15 slices

200g/7oz parsnips (about
   3 small parsnips),
   scrubbed
1 tsp cardamom seeds
250g/9oz/2 cups plain
   (all-purpose) flour or
   sifted spelt flour
200g/7oz/1 cup caster
   (superfine) sugar (or
   coconut sugar)
3 tbsp psyllium husk
4 tsp baking powder
½ tsp salt
350ml/12fl oz/scant 1½
   cups unsweetened oat
   milk
150ml/5fl oz/⅔ cup
   rapeseed (canola) oil

Cashew frosting

170g/6oz/1¼ cups cashew
   nuts
5 soft dates, pitted
½ tsp vanilla powder
finely grated zest of 1
   lemon, plus juice of ½
   lemon

Quick frosting

300g/11oz plant-based
   cream cheese
100g/3½oz/generous ¾
   cup icing (confectio-
   ners') sugar
1–2 tsp lemon juice
½ tsp vanilla powder

The first time I baked a parsnip cake was a late
summer day many years ago when my grandmother
and her sisters came to visit. It was a great success
and I've baked it several times since – nowadays
it's completely plant based. I've suggested two
alternative frostings, one blended from cashew
nuts and a quick version using shop-bought cream
cheese. Both are equally delicious!

Cake

— Preheat the oven to 180°C/350°F/Gas 4. Line a 20 x 35
   cm/8 x 14in cake tin with baking parchment.
— Grate the parsnips using the fine side of the grater (keep
   the skin on). Crush the cardamom seeds using a pestle and
   mortar. Mix together all the ingredients for the cake batter.
— Pour the batter into the prepared tin. Bake for 45 minutes,
   or until a thin skewer comes out clean when inserted into
   the middle of the cake. Leave the cake to cool completely
   before adding the frosting.

Cashew frosting

— Soak the cashew nuts in water for at least 5 hours, then
   drain.
— Put all the ingredients into a powerful food processor or
   high-speed blender, add 100ml/3½fl oz/scant ½ cup water
   and blend until smooth. You may need to add a little more
   water to achieve a spreadable consistency.
— Spread the frosting over the cake and leave to set in the
   fridge for at least 2 hours before cutting into slices.

Quick frosting

— Put all the ingredients into a bowl and stir together until
   smooth. Spread over the cake and, if possible, leave in the
   fridge for a while before serving.

143

LEMON FALAFEL WITH YELLOW PEAS

Serves 4

250g/9oz dried yellow
peas/split peas
2 brown onions, quartered
2 large handfuls fresh
parsley
4 garlic cloves, grated
grated zest of 1 lemon,
plus 1 tbsp juice
55g/2oz/scant ½ cup
plain (all-purpose) flour
or 65g/2¼oz/scant ½
cup rice flour
black sesame seeds
rapeseed (canola) oil for
frying or baking
salt and black pepper

In Sweden, we have a long history of eating yellow peas: they are filling, nutritious and could easily be stored for a long time. In modern times, dried peas have gone through a renaissance as dishes such as falafel and hummus have become everyday staples. I often use yellow peas in place of chickpeas (garbanzos) – since they are easily grown up here in the north, we can eat local produce even if the recipe inspiration comes from further away. If you buy split yellow peas, they need less soaking time.

— Soak the peas for at least 12 hours, preferably 24 hours, or according to the instructions on the pack.

— If you want to bake rather than fry the falafel, preheat the oven to 200°C/400°F/Gas 6. Line a baking sheet with baking parchment.

— Strain off the soaking water and leave the peas to drain. Put the peas in a food processor together with the onions and parsley and blend to a coarse paste. Transfer to a large bowl and add the garlic, lemon zest and juice, flour, and plenty of salt and pepper. Mix well, taste and adjust the flavours if needed.

— With damp hands, shape the mixture into about 20 balls and then roll them in sesame seeds. Fry the falafel balls in a generous amount of oil until golden brown all over, or place them on the lined baking sheet, drizzle with oil and bake for about 35 minutes. Shake the tray after 20 minutes to ensure the balls get a nice crust all the way around. Serve hot.

SALSA AND GUACAMOLE

——

Serves 4

Salsa

5 tomatoes, roughly
    chopped
1 yellow (bell) pepper,
    halved, deseeded and
    chopped
½ brown onion, thinly
    sliced
1 jalapeño, finely chopped
1 red chilli, finely chopped
2 tbsp rapeseed (canola)
    oil
salt and black pepper

Guacamole

2 very ripe avocados
1 shallot, finely chopped
½ red chilli, finely
    chopped, or 1 tsp
    sambal oelek
8 cherry tomatoes, diced
1 large handful fresh
    coriander (cilantro),
    chopped
juice of ½ lime or lemon
salt and black pepper

This salsa is cooked in the oven – meaning it will have a lightly roasted flavour and a lovely texture once the vegetables are stirred together. The guacamole isn't cooked at all, of course, but I have included it here as it's a perfect partner to salsa. Either or both of these dips go really well with the wrap fillings on page 148. The guacamole is also wonderful on toast.

Salsa
— Preheat the oven to 200°C/400°F/Gas 6.
— Put all the vegetables in a baking dish or roasting pan, drizzle with the oil and season with salt and pepper. Roast for 20–30 minutes. When the tomatoes start to release their liquid and the vegetables have started to colour, they are done.
— Stir the vegetables together to crush the tomatoes, until you have a texture like a chunky sauce or dip.

Guacamole
— Halve the avocados, remove the stones and scoop the flesh into a bowl. Add the shallot and chilli or sambal oelek and mash together using a fork.
— Fold the diced tomatoes and coriander into the avocado dip. Squeeze in lime or lemon juice and season to taste with salt and pepper.

BEAN SALSA, CHICKPEA FILLING, SESAME SAUCE

I love wrap food! Serve these tasty fillings in tortillas or in little cups or wraps made from lettuce or cabbage leaves, and drizzle with a little chilli sauce if you like.

Serves 4

Black bean salsa

2 brown onions, sliced
1 green (bell) pepper, de-seeded and chopped
85g/3oz/generous ¾ cup chopped celery
vegetable oil for frying
1 tsp ground cinnamon
½ tsp ground cumin
3 tbsp tomato purée (tomato paste)
425g/15oz/2½ cups cooked black beans, or 2 x 400g/14oz cans, drained
2 handfuls fresh coriander (cilantro), chopped
1 tsp lemon
salt and black pepper

Roasted chickpea filling

600g/1lb 5oz mixed root vegetables, e.g. carrots, potatoes, beetroot (beets)
200g/7oz/1¼ cups cooked chickpeas (garbanzos), or 400g/14oz can, drained
2 tbsp olive oil
1 tsp cayenne pepper
2 tsp paprika
½ tsp ground cumin
1 garlic clove, grated

Sesame sauce

1 garlic clove, grated
3½ tbsp tahini
3 tbsp olive oil
1 tsp lemon juice

Black bean salsa

— Gently fry the onions, pepper and celery in a little oil with some salt and pepper until the onions are thoroughly soft and have started to colour.
— Add the cinnamon and cumin and fry for 1 minute. Stir in the tomato purée and fry for another minute. Add the beans and fry for a couple of minutes until the beans are heated through. Remove from the heat, stir in the coriander and lemon juice, taste and adjust the seasoning if necessary.

Roasted chickpea filling

— Preheat the oven to 225°C/425°F/Gas 7.
— Scrub or peel the root vegetables, cut into chunks, place in an oiled roasting pan and roast for 20 minutes.
— Mix the chickpeas with the olive oil, spices and garlic and pour everything over the root vegetables. Roast for a further 10–15 minutes or until the vegetables are nicely browned. Season to taste with salt and pepper.

Sesame sauce

— Blend all the ingredients together, with salt and pepper to taste. Add 1 tablespoon water at a time (you may need 2–3 tablespoons in total) and blend between each addition until you've got a good consistency.

FRITTATA

—

Serves 4

Vegetables

700g/1lb 9oz potatoes
    and squash
150g/5½oz beetroot
    (beets)
vegetable oil for frying
3 tbsp chopped fresh
    sage
8 large cavolo nero leaves
3 small red onions, cut
    into large chunks
2–3 garlic cloves, grated
salt and black pepper

Frittata batter

75g/2½oz/generous ¾
    cup gram (chickpea/
    garbanzo) flour
3½ tbsp soya or oat
    whipping cream
1 tbsp baking powder
1 tbsp apple cider vinegar
2 tbsp nutritional yeast
½ tsp ground fenugreek
½ tsp salt

To serve

salad leaves, with
    slow-roasted tomatoes
    if you have some

A frittata is a rustic Italian omelette that I make in the oven, using root vegetables, squash and sage. Squash works particularly well as it gets really silky and buttery in the oven.

— Preheat the oven to 180°C/350°F/Gas 4. Line a baking dish or roasting pan (approx. 22 x 32cm/8½ x 13in) with baking parchment.
— Scrub the potatoes (and peel them if you like), squash and beetroots. Cut into bite-sized chunks. Fry the root vegetables in oil in a large frying pan (skillet) together with the sage and some salt and pepper until they start to soften and brown.
— Pick the leaves off the cavolo nero stalks and tear into smaller pieces. Add the onions, cavolo nero and garlic to the frying pan and fry gently for a few minutes, until the onion starts to look glossy.
— Put the gram flour into a large bowl. Add 200ml/7fl oz/ generous ¾ cup water and the remaining ingredients for the batter and whisk until smooth. Pour half into the lined baking dish or roasting pan, then spoon in the vegetables and pour over the rest of the batter. Bake the frittata for 20–30 minutes or until the batter has set; use a thin skewer to test that the centre is cooked.
— Serve with a salad.

INDEX

First published in the United Kingdom in 2020 by
Pavilion
43 Great Ormond Street
London
WC1N 3HZ

Copyright © Pavilion Books Company Ltd

Original title: Värmande vego
Text and photography © Karoline Jönsson and Norstedts,
First published by Norstedts, Sweden, in 2019
Published by agreement with Norstedts Agency.

ISBN 978-1-911663-14-0

A CIP catalogue record for this book is available
from the British Library.

10 9 8 7 6 5 4 3 2 1

Photography: Karoline Jönsson
Design: Kristin Lidström
Reproduction: JK Morris AB, Värnamo
Printed and bound by Toppan Leefung Ltd., China
www.pavilionbooks.com